Incredible True
Adventures

THE FIRST SOLO FLIGHT
ACROSS THE ATLANTIC

BY CAITLIN MCANENEY

Gareth Stevens
PUBLISHING

Please visit our website, www.garethstevens.com. For a free color catalog of all our high-quality books, call toll free 1-800-542-2595 or fax 1-877-542-2596.

Library of Congress Cataloging-in-Publication Data

McAneney, Caitlin.
The first solo flight across the Atlantic / by Caitlin McAneney.
p. cm. — (Incredible true adventures)
Includes index.
ISBN 978-1-4824-2034-0 (pbk.)
ISBN 978-1-4824-2033-3 (6-pack)
ISBN 978-1-4824-2035-7 (library binding)
1. Transatlantic flights — Juvenile literature. I. McAneney, Caitlin. II. Title.
TL531. M384 2015
629.13—d23

First Edition

Published in 2015 by
Gareth Stevens Publishing
111 East 14th Street, Suite 349
New York, NY 10003

Copyright © 2015 Gareth Stevens Publishing

Designer: Andrea Davison-Bartolotta
Editor: Kristen Rajczak

Photo credits: Cover, p. 1 S. Borisov/Shutterstock.com; p. 4 Dorling Kindersley/Vetta/Getty Images; p. 5 Science & Society Picture Library/SSPL/Getty Images; pp. 6, 7 LOC.gov; p. 8 Alan R. Hawley collection/Wikimedia Commons; p. 9 Time Life Pictures/National Archives/Time & Life Pictures/Getty Images; pp. 10–11 Time Life Pictures/Mansell/Time & Life Pictures/Getty Images; pp. 12, 14, 15, 21 Keystone-France/Gamma-Keystone/Getty Images; pp. 13, 18 NY Daily News Archive/Getty Images; p. 16 Leemage/Universal Images Group/Getty Images; p. 17 (main) Topical Press Agency/Getty Images; p. 17 (globe) rtguest/Shutterstock.com; p. 17 (airplane) Alexandr III/Shutterstock.com; p. 19 Central Press/Getty Images; pp. 22–23 Petrified Collection/The Image Bank/Getty Images; p. 24 Pictures Inc./The LIFE Picture Collection/Time & Life Pictures/Getty Images; p. 25 NASA/Photo Researchers/Getty Images; p. 26 Josef Hanus/Shutterstock.com; p. 27 Tom Hollyman/Photo Researchers/Getty Images; p. 29 Douglas Keister/Hulton Archive/Getty Images.

Printed in the United States of America

CPSIA compliance information: Batch #CW15GS: For further information contact Gareth Stevens, New York, New York at 1-800-542-2595.

Contents »»»»»»»»»»

Words in the glossary appear in **bold** type the first time they are used in the text.

Sky's the Limit!

Centuries ago, great explorers sailed the oceans and discovered new lands, mapping the unknown world. In the 1900s, people took to a new **frontier**—the sky. **Pilots** became the true explorers of the 20th century.

Orville and Wilbur Wright built and flew the first successful engine-powered airplane in 1903. Soon, more airplanes were built, and more pilots were trained to fly them. As airplanes improved, flights became longer and a question formed: Who would be the first to cross the Atlantic Ocean? A flight over the world's second-largest ocean was a deadly challenge, and it would take a true adventurer to try it.

The Wright Brothers

The Wright brothers built glider planes from 1900 to 1902 and brought them to the windy coastal area of Kitty Hawk, North Carolina. At Kitty Hawk, they broke a record by gliding 620 feet (189 m) in 1902. Their engine-powered airplane had special wings, an engine, and a **propeller**. Orville flew it successfully on December 17, 1903, for 12 seconds!

Wright brothers' plane, 1903

The first planes were gliders, which used only air to stay up and had to be very light. The Wright brothers built a plane that used the air, but was also powered by an engine.

Looking Up

The first pilot to successfully cross the Atlantic Ocean from New York to Paris alone was Charles Lindbergh. Lindbergh was born on February 4, 1902, in Detroit, Michigan. He split his childhood between Washington, DC, where his father was a US congressman, and Little Falls, Minnesota. Much of Lindbergh's childhood was spent on his family's farm on the Mississippi River.

Lindbergh liked to camp, hunt, and explore in nature. He also liked to fix things, and he started driving a car at only 11 years old! He discovered his love for airplanes at a young age after hearing one of the first planes fly over his house.

Charles Lindbergh (left), 1925

Brave Young Pilot

At only 20 years old, Lindbergh decided to go to flying school. He'd never liked regular school, but flying school was interesting and exciting for him. He learned how planes worked and how to fix them. That year, he learned how to fly, walk on an airplane's wings, and even **parachute!**

Lindbergh went to see an airplane show in Virginia in June 1912. He watched excitedly as an airplane took off. He couldn't wait to be a pilot someday!

HITTING THE SKY

Charles Lindbergh made his first solo flight in 1923, and he was soon hooked on flying. The following year, he went to San Antonio, Texas, to begin US Army flying school. He was the best pilot in his class! In 1926, he found a job flying mail between Chicago, Illinois, and St. Louis, Missouri. He was the first airmail pilot to fly that route.

At age 24, Lindbergh was already breaking records and paving his own path. When he heard about a challenge to cross the Atlantic, he knew he'd have to try.

The Orteig Prize

Raymond Orteig was an important New York City businessman. In 1919, he offered to award $25,000 to the first person to fly nonstop from New York to Paris. It wasn't until 1926 that Lindbergh considered the possibility of winning the prize. More than the money, Lindbergh wanted to make people aware of the new possibilities of **aviation**.

Lindbergh and Orteig ❯

Here, Lindbergh (right) helps load mail for his first flight from St. Louis to Chicago for the US Postal Service (USPS). The USPS started flying mail around the nation in 1918.

PIONEER PILOTS

Charles Lindbergh wasn't the first pilot to cross the Atlantic Ocean. But his goal was to be the first to fly from New York to mainland Europe solo in one flight. Others had attempted the **transatlantic** flight before him, and some died trying.

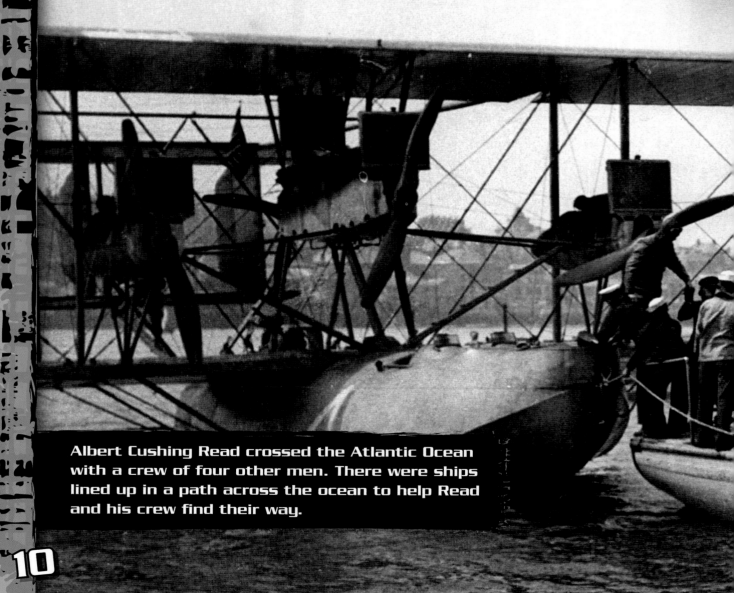

Albert Cushing Read crossed the Atlantic Ocean with a crew of four other men. There were ships lined up in a path across the ocean to help Read and his crew find their way.

On May 8, 1919, American pilot Albert Cushing Read and his crew left New York for England in a flying boat, or a plane that could land on water. The flight took 23 days, and there were stops to get fuel and rest. Englishmen John Alcock and Arthur Whitten Brown made the first nonstop transatlantic flight in June 1919, from Newfoundland, Canada, to Ireland.

Flight Failures

Crossing the Atlantic Ocean was very risky! In May 1919, Australian pilot Harry Hawker tried to fly across the Atlantic, but after 14 hours, he and his partner had to crash-land in the water and return home by boat. French pilots Charles Nungesser and François Coli weren't as lucky. In May 1927, their plane crashed and was never found.

CHASING THE PRIZE

Despite the challenges Lindbergh faced, he believed that he could do what other people couldn't. He talked to a group of businessmen in St. Louis, and they decided to give him money to help make his dream a reality.

With the money, Lindbergh had to build a plane. He wanted a single engine **monoplane**. Other pilots attempting the transatlantic flight had used more than one engine. Lindbergh named his plane the *Spirit of St. Louis* after the location of the businessmen who funded his trip. He was one step closer to winning the Orteig Prize, but it was a race against time!

Lindbergh working on the *Spirit of St. Louis*

Lindbergh gave Ryan Airlines only 60 days to build his famous one-engine plane! Other pilots were also chasing the prize, so Lindbergh didn't have a lot of time.

Breaking a Record

On May 10, 1927, Lindbergh took his first long flight in the *Spirit of St. Louis*. He flew from San Diego, California, to St. Louis. The 1,500-mile (2,414 km) journey took only 14 hours and 25 minutes, and he flew it nonstop. He'd broken a flight record before he even started his transatlantic flight!

READY FOR TAKEOFF!

After the long flight from San Diego to St. Louis, and then another from St. Louis to New York, Lindbergh had to get ready for his longest flight yet. He packed water, sandwiches, and 450 gallons (1,700 l) of fuel.

His plane was heavy—and that would be a big challenge. The heavier the plane, the harder it was to lift off the ground. An even greater challenge was Lindbergh's lack of sleep. He hadn't been able to sleep the night before, and he had 33 hours of flying ahead of him! But despite the challenges, this 25-year-old mail pilot was about to make history.

Takeoff

Some people called Lindberg the "flying fool." He was young, a solo pilot, and flying a small plane. On top of that, the weather was bad in the days before the flight. But on May 20, 1927, Lindbergh sped down the runway anyway. His plane, heavy with extra fuel, took flight just in time to miss a bunch of telephone wires!

Lindbergh's last words before takeoff were: "What do you say? Let's try it."

A Historic Flight

The flight from New York to Paris was about 3,600 miles (5,794 km) without stopping. Lindbergh flew through the darkness over the ocean, sometimes through fog and even sleet. He knew turning back wasn't an option.

The flight across the ocean was long, but finally Lindbergh spotted the coast of Ireland. He crossed Ireland and England and finally made it to Paris. He circled around the Eiffel Tower, looking at what awaited him. In New York, a group of about 500 people had sent him off. In Paris, there were more than 100,000 people cheering for him as he landed at Le Bourget Field.

Worldwide Fame

Lindbergh's flight brought him worldwide fame. A very tired Lindbergh greeted the huge crowd in Paris from the balcony of the American **Embassy**. The president of France gave him a Legion of Honor pin. He was on the front page of newspapers around the world!

LE PETIT JOURNAL

HEBDOMADAIRE - 38ᵉ Année
61, rue Lafayette, Paris

ILLUSTRE

5 Juin 1927 - N° 1902
PRIX : 50 CENTIMES

NUMÉRO SPÉCIAL

Spirit of St. Louis

DE NEW-YORK À PARIS EN AVION
"Je suis Charles Lindbergh !"

Lindbergh's flight path

Paris

New York

Lindbergh had made history with his flight. He was carried through the crowd in Paris and honored like a king!

CELEBRITY PILOT

People around the world were talking about Lindbergh's flight, and in America, he got the homecoming he deserved. When he returned to New York City, there was a huge parade in his honor with millions of people lining the streets. President Calvin Coolidge gave him the Distinguished Flying Cross, a great award.

Lindbergh was now a **celebrity** pilot! He went on a tour of 92 cities with his plane, the *Spirit of St. Louis*. Many cities had their own special parade for him. His speeches on this tour helped to get people excited about the future of flying.

Before the flight, people called Lindbergh the "flying fool," but after the flight, they called him the "Lone Eagle" and "Lucky Lindy."

Ticker-Tape Parades

Ticker-tape parades are an important part of New York City history. These parades used shredded ticker tape, which was a long piece of paper with messages printed on it, like confetti is used today. The parades honored a special event or person. The ticker-tape parade for Charles Lindbergh was held on June 13, 1927. There were nearly 4 million people there, and the mayor of New York City gave Lindbergh a special medal.

Meeting His Match

Lindbergh was truly a world traveler. After he finished his tour of the United States, he flew to Central and South America. On his travels, he met Anne Spencer Morrow, and Lindbergh fell in love with her. They were married in 1929 and became one of the most famous couples in America.

Anne and Charles Lindbergh took on the job of charting new flight routes across the world. They even flew as far as China and Japan together in a single-engine plane! Anne helped Lindbergh by **navigating** and operating the radio, and she was even a copilot. They flew over 40,000 miles (64,374 km) together.

The Price of Fame

On March 1, 1932, Lindbergh's son was kidnapped. The kidnapper had left a note asking for money in return for the baby. After a long hunt for the kidnapper, led mostly by Lindbergh himself, the baby was found. He had died. The trial of Bruno Richard Hauptmann, the possible kidnapper, became known as the "trial of the century."

Anne and Charles Lindbergh seemed to be a perfect match. She was the first woman in the United States to earn her glider pilot's license!

LINDBERGH IN WWII

Lindbergh and his wife moved to Europe just before World War II (1939–1945). The US military sent Lindbergh to Germany to see how advanced the German military aviation program was. His reports helped the United States prepare for war.

During World War II, Lindbergh worked with Henry Ford to build bomber planes. He also played a key role in **designing** the first airline routes. Later, he taught pilots serving in the Pacific how to fly better and use less fuel. He could lengthen their flights by nearly 500 miles (805 km) with his flying **techniques**! Lindbergh also flew more than 50 missions with the US military.

Military Flights

Throughout World War I (1914–1918), early fighter planes, bomber planes, and flying boats were developed. These small planes usually carried one person. By World War II, because of the advances in flight, airplanes were faster, could go much farther, and could carry more people. Transatlantic and transpacific flights were important because World War II was fought around the world.

In World War I, US soldiers spent much of their time living in and fighting out of trenches, or pits in the ground. In World War II, because of the progress in aviation, more soldiers fought in the air.

THE FUTURE OF FLYING

By making the first solo transatlantic flight, Charles Lindbergh made it possible for others to challenge the limits of aviation.

The 1930s saw the first transatlantic flights to carry **passengers**. In 1931, Clyde Pangborn and Hugh Herndon Jr. became the first pilots to fly nonstop across the Pacific Ocean. That same year, Wiley Post and Harold Gatty flew around the world, making many stops. World War II advanced the course of aviation, and in 1949, Captain James Gallagher circled the world nonstop! In the decades that followed, commercial flight became a normal way to get around.

Lady Lindy

In 1928, Amelia Earhart became the first woman to fly across the Atlantic Ocean. Earhart wasn't the pilot, however, and she didn't like being "baggage." So in 1932, Amelia Earhart became the first woman to pilot a transatlantic flight. Earhart was nicknamed "Lady Lindy" because, like Lindbergh, she'd taken one huge step for aviation.

Lindbergh (standing at left) helped set the stage for rocket research, the future of flying. In 1968, he and some of the earliest astronauts, as well as President Lyndon B. Johnson (standing at right), signed a document honoring the manned space flights of Apollo 7 and Apollo 8.

COMMERCIAL FLIGHT

Commercial flights carry passengers or goods for profit. Lindbergh believed in the possibilities of commercial flight from the beginning of his career.

Lindbergh worked as chairman of the Technical Committee for Transcontinental Air Transport starting in 1928. His job was to chart flight routes across the country, and the airline became known as the "Lindbergh Line." After World War II, he also worked as an advisor to Pan American Airways. He found new routes and tested planes that could be used by the airline. Lindbergh was responsible for making sure commercial aviation used the best airplanes and the most direct routes.

Flights Today

Charles Lindbergh imagined a world where people could get anywhere by flying. Today, there are more than 87,000 flights in the United States each day, and about 29,000 of those are commercial flights. There are about 9,000 airports worldwide that serve commercial passengers. In 2013, about 743 million people flew in the United States alone!

By 1950, the transatlantic route was the most traveled air route in the world! This picture shows the cockpit of a Pan American flight in the 1950s.

LINDBERGH'S LEGACY

Charles Lindbergh spent his last years in Maui, Hawaii, until his death on August 26, 1974. In his 72 years, he lived through most of mankind's greatest successes in aviation. He had played a huge part in the advancement of air travel and, because of that, space travel.

Famous Flights

December 1903: The Wright brothers fly the first successful engine-powered airplane.

May 1919: Albert Cushing Read pilots a flying boat across the Atlantic Ocean, which takes 23 days.

June 1919: John Alcock and Arthur Whitten Brown make the first nonstop transatlantic flight from Newfoundland to Ireland in about 16 hours.

May 1927: Charles Lindbergh makes the first nonstop solo flight from New York to Paris in just over 33 hours.

June 1928: Amelia Earhart becomes the first woman passenger on a transatlantic flight.

June 1931: Wiley Post and Harold Gatty fly around the world, making 14 stops.

October 1931: Clyde Pangborn and Hugh Herndon Jr. make the first nonstop flight across the Pacific Ocean from Japan to Washington State.

May 1932: Amelia Earhart becomes the first woman to pilot a transatlantic flight.

July 1933: Wiley Post makes the first solo flight around the world, in 7 days and 18 hours.

February 1949: Captain James Gallagher circles the world nonstop with a crew of 14 men, taking 94 hours.

Lindbergh was a true explorer who changed the future of America. He explored and mapped flight paths across the United States and overseas. He was an expert pilot whose **legacy** inspired pilots to push the limits of sky and space. Most importantly, he made people excited about the possibilities of flight, revving America's engine toward the open sky.

Lindbergh Lives On

Charles Lindbergh lives on in the knowledge he left behind. In his lifetime, he wrote seven books to share his life, knowledge, and experiences. The most famous book is titled *The Spirit of St. Louis*. Published in 1953, this book tells the true story of his first transatlantic flight.

Lindbergh's grave

Lindbergh loved the natural beauty of Hawaii. He fell ill in New York City and took his last flight just before his death, going home to Maui.

Glossary >>>>>>>>>>>>

aviation: the act, practice, or science of flying airplanes

celebrity: a person who is famous

design: to draw plans for something new

embassy: the official home of a country's ambassador, or someone who represents a country in another nation

frontier: a new field to be developed

legacy: something that is passed down from someone

monoplane: an airplane with only one main support surface

navigate: to find one's way

parachute: to drop from an aircraft with a special cloth that slows the fall

passenger: a person who does not drive or pilot, but travels in a car, bus, train, or aircraft

pilot: someone who flies aircraft

propeller: a device with spinning blades that makes an airplane move forward

technique: a certain way of doing something

transatlantic: crossing the Atlantic Ocean

Books

Saddlebrook Educational Publishing. *Charles Lindbergh.* Irvine, CA: Saddleback Educational Publishing, 2008.

Schraff, Anne. *Daredevil American Heroes of Exploration and Flight.* Berkeley Heights, NJ: Enslow, 2013.

Websites

Aviation for Kids: Timeline
www.aviation-for-kids.com/time-line.html
Check out this timeline to learn more about major events in the history of aviation.

Lindbergh Flies the Atlantic, 1927
www.eyewitnesstohistory.com/lindbergh.htm
Read about Charles Lindbergh's historic flight in his own words.

The Spirit of St. Louis
www.charleslindbergh.com/plane/
Learn more about Charles Lindbergh's famous airplane, the *Spirit of St. Louis*!

Index »»»»»»»»»»»